DISCOVER
The Kingdom of Kush

by Barbara Brannon

Table of Contents

Introduction

Kush was important. Kush was an important **civilization**.

▲ Kush was a great civilization.

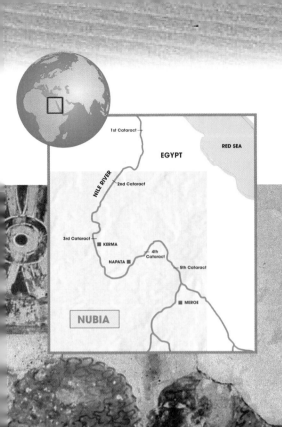

civilization

crops

deserts

farms

iron

Kush

See the Glossary
on page 22.

3

What Was Kush Like?

Kush had dry land. Kush had **deserts**.

▲ This desert was in Kush.

Kush had the Nile River. Kush had the
Nile River Valley.

▲ This valley was in Kush.
This river was in Kush.

Kush had good land. Kush had **crops**.

▼ barley

▼ wheat

▲ These crops grew in Kush.

Kush had towns.

▲ This town was in Kush.

Kush had cities.

▲ This city was in Kush.

Kush had pyramids.

▲ This pyramid was in Kush.

Kush had temples.

IT'S A FACT

Elephants lived in temples in Kush.

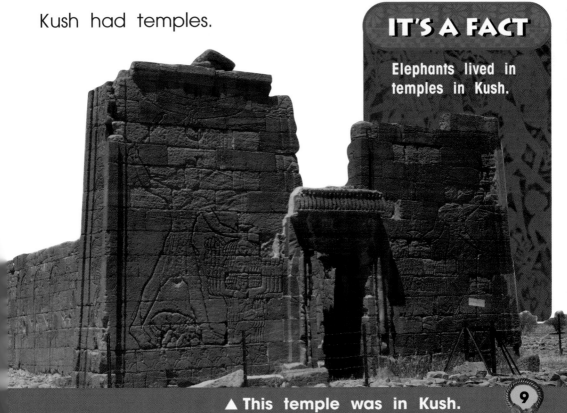

▲ This temple was in Kush.

How Did the People Live in Kush?

Some people were rich. Some people were kings. Some people were queens.

▲ Kush had kings and queens.

Some people were farmers.

▲ Kush had farmers.

Some people were builders.

▲ Kush had builders.

Some people were artisans.

▲ Kush had art.

IT'S A FACT

Artisans were people
who made things.
Artisans in Kush made
beautiful things.

Some people were warriors.

IT'S A FACT

People of Kush were fighters. They fought with other countries.

▲ Kush had warriors.

Why Was Kush Important?

The people had **farms**.

▲ Kush had farms.

The people had **iron**. The people had gold.

▲ Kush had iron.

▲ Kush had gold.

The people had a way to write.

THE MEROITIC ALPHABET

Hieroglyph	Cursive Letter	Phonetic Value	Hieroglyph	Cursive Letter	Phonetic Value
	ς2	a		⸝	l
	ς	e		▽	h
	✦	o		⸝	h
	/	i		⸝	s, s
	///	y		V//	se
	⸝	w		⸝	k
	μ	b		Ṗ	q
	Z	p		⸝	t
	⸝	m		/4	te
	⸝	n		⸝	to
	⸝	ne		⸝	d
	ω	r			

▲ Kush had writing.

DID YOU KNOW?

Today no one can speak Kush. No one can read Kush writing.

Conclusion

Kush was a great civilization.

▲ Kush was an important civilization.

Concept Map

Kush

What Was Kush Like?

- dry land
- deserts
- Nile River
- Nile River Valley
- good land
- crops
- towns
- cities
- pyramids
- temples

How Did the People Live?	Why Was Kush Important?
rich people	farms
kings	iron
farmers	gold
builders	writing
artisans	
warriors	

Glossary

civilization a group of people that share ideas about living together

*Kush was a great **civilization**.*

crops plants grown for food

*Kush had **crops**.*

deserts dry, hot lands

*Kush had **deserts**.*

farms land used to grow plants and raise animals

*The people had **farms**.*

iron a hard metal

*The people had **iron**.*

Kush a civilization in Africa

***Kush** was a great civilization.*

23

Index